Greg De

THE HELLBOX

Oxford   New York

OXFORD UNIVERSITY PRESS

1998

Oxford University Press, Great Clarendon Street, Oxford OX2 6DP

Oxford New York

Athens Auckland Bangkok Bogota Bombay Buenos Aires
Calcutta Cape Town Dar es Salaam Delhi Florence Hong Kong Istanbul
Karachi Kuala Lumpur Madras Madrid Melbourne Mexico City
Nairobi Paris Singapore Taipei Tokyo Toronto Warsaw

and associated companies in
Berlin Ibadan

Oxford is a trade mark of Oxford University Press

First published in Oxford Poets
as an Oxford University Press paperback 1998

British Library Cataloguing in Publication Data
Data available

Library of Congress Cataloging in Publication Data

Delanty, Greg, 1958–
The hellbox / Greg Delanty.
p. cm. — (Oxford poets)
1. Fathers and sons—Poetry. 2. Printing—Poetry
I. Title. II. Series
PR6054.E397H45 1998 821'.914—dc21 97–34624

ISBN 0–19–288088–8

1 3 5 7 9 10 8 6 4 2

Typeset by George Hammond Design
Printed in Hong Kong

THE HELLBOX

By the same author:

Cast in the Fire (1986)
Southward (1992)
American Wake (1995)

Acknowledgements

Anthology of Magazine Verse & Yearbook of American Poetry 1995/1996, Books Ireland, Cimarron Review, College English, Compost, The Examiner, Fortnight, Irish in America, the *Irish Review, The Irish Times,* the *Kenyon Review,* the *Literary Review, Pivot, Ploughshares, Poetry Ireland Review,* RTÉ Radio, *Shenandoah,* the *Southern Review, A Time of Grace—Edmund Rice and the Presentation Tradition of Education,* the Crawford Municipal Art Gallery.

'The Compositor' appeared in the *Atlantic Monthly* in August 1995.

'Striped Ink' won the RTÉ Radio 1 Austin Clarke Centenary Poetry Competition sponsored by RTÉ Television and Radio.

I'd like particularly to thank the following people and organizations for their assistance: The Heinrich Böll Foundation; Charles Baraw; John Bourke; David Cavanagh; Bonnie Christenson; Michael Coffey; The Coolatore House Foundation; David Curzon; Louis de Paor; Patricia Ferreira; Bob Fricke; Fred Kenneally; Gregory O'Donoghue; Robert O'Donoghue; Ghita Orth; John O'Shea; Christopher Ricks; The Shelburne Printing Museum; St Michael's College; Katherine Washburn; Robert Welch; Jonathan Williams, Literary Agent; and The Wolfers-O'Neill Literary Foundation. I also consulted Joseph Moxon's *Mechanick Exercises on the Whole Art of Printing.* In the dedication of 'The Printer's Devil', CND stands for the Campaign for Nuclear Disarmament. 'Modern Times' was written in May 1995. The epigraph of 'We Will Not Play the Harp Backward Now, No' was taken from Marianne Moore's 'Spenser's Ireland'. The editors of the *Norton Anthology of Modern Poetry* annotated these lines of Moore: 'The harp is the symbol of Ireland. To play it backward is to be sentimental about the past.'

Especially for Patricia Ferreira

Contents

THE COMPOSING ROOM

The Compositor

Perhaps it's the smell of printing ink
sets me off out of memory's jumbled font
or maybe it's the printer's lingo
as he relates how phrases came about.

How for instance: *mind your p's & q's*
has as much to do with pints & quarts
and the printer's renown for drink
as it has with those descenders.

But I don't say anything about
how I discovered where *widows & orphans*
and *out of sorts* came from the day my father
unnoticed and unexpectedly set *30*

on the bottom of his compositor's page
and left me mystified about the origins
of that end, how to measure a line gauge
and how, since he was first to go,

he slowly and without a word
turned from himself into everyone
as we turn into that last zero
before finally passing on to the stoneman.

The Cure

to my father

I drop into the printers and graft
to you with my hangover on hearing
the tall drinking tales of your craft
from an apprentice of yours, latching

on to the old typesetter days like myself.
He swore he could write a book.
I thought of how you were partial yourself
to a jorum or two, but you would look

down on my pint-swaggering and remind me
you kept your drinking to Saturday night,
bar births, weddings, deaths and maybe
the odd quick one if the company was right.

And for the most part I keep to that too,
but last night was a night I broke
and went on the rantan from bar to
bar on my tod, jawing with whatever bloke,

solving the world's problems drink by drink
and cigarette by cigarette, swigging
and puffing away the whole lousy stink.
You nagged away in my head about smoking

and how the butts did away with you.
But I swear the way I stood there
and yakkety-yakked, slagged and blew
smoke into the smoke-shrouded air,

coughing your smoker's cough,
I thought that you had turned into me
or I into you. I laughed your laugh
and then, knowing how you loved company,

I refused to quit the bar and leave you alone
or leave myself alone or whoever we were.
I raised my glass to your surprise return.
And now I hear you guffaw once more

as your apprentice continues to recount
printers' drink lore and asks if I know
comps at Signature O got a complimentary pint.
I joust our way out the door repeating *O O O*.

Passing the Evergreen Bar

i.m. Raymond Cunningham and Danny Delanty

Suddenly I'm back all those Saturday nights ago,
    dropping in on you as you light each other up
    and call for attention only when you call.
Your palaver is all Eagle Printing shop talk,
    fixing dancing words on the pub's correcting stone
    before the whole works is choked and broken up.
Now you set the good old days up again, and I,
    a printer's devil, pie that dumped stick,
    inserting how those times were as foul as today's.
You each take a slug, then laugh this spirit off,
    ordering me keep my moolah for the dance as you call.
I delay heading down Summerhill to the disco's strobes,
    scraps, shifts and refusals and stay for just one
more with you, forever, in the spoiled good old days.

The Composing Room

I still see those men haphazardly standing
around the comp's floor, mostly silent,
lost in their latest urgent jobs,
looking up and down as if nodding yes

from what they call their composer's sticks
as they set inverse letters and lines
of each page that could be taken for
Greek scripture, declaring:

In the beginning was the Word and the Word
was made cold type and the Word was
coldness, darkness, shiny greyness
and light—And the Word dwelt amongst us.

*

Oh I know these men would laugh this off.
They'd say, if they simply didn't throw
their eyes to heaven, that they were just ordinary
blokes trying to keep the devil from the door,

and with luck have enough left over each week
to back a few nags, and go for a few jars.
But they can't say anything or set anything now.
They are scattered from that place that's not

the same anymore and many have left
any place we know of in this life,
calling to mind the old names for printing:
The Mysterious Craft or simply *The Mystery*.

I set them up in another city, another country
that's as far away in distance
from that city as it's far in time.
But they are still composing,

cracking the odd joke above
their sticks and galleys on some floor
of some building that is eternally busy
inside me even when I've forgotten

that I've forgotten them; forgetting
the world behind the word—
Every time I read the word *world* I wonder
is it a typo and should I delete the *l*.

*

Now again I hanker to know the quality
of each letter: the weight, the texture, the smell,
the shiny new type, the ink-dark shades of old,
the different types of type, the various sizes

within the same font, the measures in ems,
picas, points and units . . . I'd set the words up,
making something out of all this
that stays standing—All set as masterly

as the words those men set that reveal
something of the mystery behind
and within these letters and the wonder and
the darkness, but with the lightest touch.

*

And the umpteen ways things can foul up
are beyond telling. Maybe the type is off,
or the typesetter may not be up
to the work, if only out of a hangover

setting an *!* where there should be a *?*
or a *b* where there should be a *d*,
or miss aspace or a line or dingbat.
And the proofreaders don't catch the error,

passing the copy on as clean, or the make-up man
fouls the assembly page, or the stoneman errs
as he fastens the page of cold type and furniture
with the chase turning the quoin's key.

*

Not to speak of the evil eye cast by
fellow composers who are perpetually ready
to knock the words of others, or the bosses
writing on the composition: *Kill.*

Old Shades, keep my words from such eyes
and fretting about that pied world and let me go
on regardless. And even if I foul up and the stewards
are right to set *Kill* on my last page and my words

are distributed and thrown in the hellbox,
the real achievement will be that I tried to set
the words right; that I did it with much labour
and not without a font of love. But that said,

*

Grant me the skill to free the leaden words
from the words I set, undo their awkwardness,
the weight of each letter of each word
so that the words disappear, fall away

or are forgotten and what remains is the metal
of feeling and thought behind
and beyond the cast of words
dissolving in their own ink wash.

Within this solution we find ourselves,
meeting only here, through *The Mystery*,
but relieved nonetheless to meet, if only
behind the characters of one fly-boy's words.

∧

I set and reset this page,
but keep fouling each line.
It's as if the letters rage,
rebel and decline
to let any man set
down this wrong and thus
be freed himself, let
off from how typos,
word-men, typophiles,
galley slaves, typesetters,
comps set females,
like some religious order,
in their chapel's lower case,
locking women
into a tightly screwed chase.
And this went on unseen
for so long that few thought it
unjustified,
                 with their obscene
wisecracks about the spirit
school for women
or about that magazine
composed by women whose name I forget,
but that must be, I imagine,
the upside down peace sign or caret,
rather than the old hex
of the deleting, nameless X.

Mirror

Patricia storytells how as a young one,
she set the word clues of treasure hunts
back-to-front, equipping everyone
with mirrors to decipher the hints.
I recall being unable to figure out
the inverted, rubber characters
in the name stamp of my toy printing set

till I placed the bright idea of a mirror
to the type and letters turned right.
As I read, the shaving glass in a flash
caught the sun and words became light,
heliographing help is coming thru the pass,
the enemy is finally taking flight,
or the getaway's set for that night.

Bad Impression

Right now the men put aside
        their composing sticks
and settle by the hellbox
        chatting in groups
that never seem to vary
        from day to day.
Naturally, I'm anxious to fit
        in naturally,
to be considered one amongst
        metal men and composers.
I hesitate on the edge of
        the company, not sure
which group I should join,
        not wanting to be
wholly part of any. I stroll up
        to the nearest set.
My heart pistons as fast
        as a printing machine's
and my legs are as heavy
        as a case of spacers.
It's worse than approaching some
        crush on a Saturday night
to ask her for a dance
        over the disco music
that's louder than the machine floor
        in full swing.
I blurt out about
        how Cork Celtic
will kill Hibs next Sunday
        down the Box—
In the same breath I address one comp
        as the Pelé of composers.
He slowly turns and I see myself
        inverted and fouled

in the magnifying lens of his eyes
     and in all the other eyes
turned my way, justified with his.
     He turns back and continues
what he was saying, but not
     before dumping the stick
of a wisecrack they all guffaw at.
     The other backs turn
back and I'm stranded
     like an orphan line.

But now I'm not there anymore,
     and it's years later.
I'm older than many
     of those galley-slaves were then.
I walk up to the word-man
     I admire and he turns
in such a fashion.
     His party laughs at his crack
like the typesetters,
     except, they sip from wine glasses,
instead of chipped mugs, grasp slim
     volumes and never utter a foul word.
Nevertheless, they all turn aside
     or completely away
like mirrors turned to the wall
     when someone has died.

White Spirits

In the beginning, typography was denounced
as *The Black Art*. Though why or by whom
I can't exactly say.

                    Perhaps it had to do
with an invention's magic air, or the fear
that the spread of the word would undo souls—
It probably simply came down to printers
being eternally bedaubed in black ink.

Lately I've been thinking along the lines
of how certain composers set words out of
their own ink-black darkness—

                        And no matter
how strong the white spirits, they cannot
wash the ink from their hands, stained
like a weeping woman's mascara-smudged face,
or the finger-printed hands of a gangster.

The Bent Font

I

On Poetry Rejection

Today's a day I could slip in
a bent font to foul up the machine,
so I could get away, but this time
not for a christening, or a communion,
or simply a cure, but to escape the hands
writing KILL on my words,

                        setting me back,
an infant, in the stocks of my school desk
struggling to write the numeral eight.

Somehow it's as if instinctively
I sense the actual drawing
of this figure—starting as a half circle
reaching away in the opposite
direction to form an S
and then turning back
to complete the figure—is a choreograph
of the making of the configuration of a poem.

Brother Patrick leans over and my number's up.
My hand trembles too much to draw on.
He marches me to the dunce's corner.
I'm relieved my back is to everyone,
ashamed and vexed with my tears.
But what kills me most is,
while kept in late after school,
not a soul witnesses me write that 8.

On Receiving Awards

It's like being pushed into the pool of swimming
    gala days again,
the years of months training each day, slogging
    up
and down the baths from dawn until the whistle for
    school,
freestyling and butterflying enough each week to
    make Youghal
or Ringabella and back, working on style,
    breathing, kicking,
racing each other and the clock until the day
    for the Nationals,
wondering if I'd beat my traditional rival
    Williamson this year,
warning myself to stay cool when he dispatches his
    club's henchmen
over minutes before the final to call me a culchee,
    they being Dubs,
and everyone outside of Dublin, even from our
    second largest city,
or especially from our second largest city, being
    a mucker.

And now I'm preparing for the starting block,
    making windmills
of my arms, shaking out my already shaking hands
    and legs,
adjusting my goggles, praying to trounce all comers
    as they pray the same prayer.

All I remember next is gliding out of the last
        tumble and seeing I'm ahead
of Williamson and Aidan Buckley, knowing
        they'll never catch me.
After I touch home I stand up elated, relieved,
        superior,
shaking hands with the others, ignoring downcast
        heads.
I feign modesty, dry myself, don my club's mandarin
        track suit.
As we parade to the winners' presentation, waving to
        the applauding spectators,
I'm already aware of rancour brewing in the echelons of
        the gallery's clapping.
On the tiers of the podium our glaring medals
        hang from tricolour ribbons,
brandished like the eyes of Cyclops turned against
        each other.

Modern Times

for Seán Dunne

I've a notion, instead of entering the hereafter
or turning into some mythical tree,
the spirits of dead shakers enter
the wood they fashioned with such severity.

The frigid, upright, spiny furniture
seems to withdraw as we intrude on each room
set so sparsely in this New Hampshire
ghost town that I can't imagine calling home.

And coming on their antique printer's shop,
with galley pages of *The Shaker Manifesto*
locked by the quoins so no character could drop,
I long for the security of such words.

But I've lost my quoin's key
and all my shaken words fall uneven.

The Printer's Devil

to the Cork CND Office

My father led me around the composer's room
and forecast comps were for the hellbox
as they set up inverse words.
He showed me how to space the space between
lines, fix leads and distribute images.

One Christmas he bought me a printer's set
like the one I use now to stamp envelopes
Compliments of this political party
or that, labouring as your apprentice to set
the upside-down, backward world upright.

But I haven't the skill to make our demons,
or the knack of stacking the characters
of politicians the right way
round and I keep smudging between the lines.

Striped Ink

I

I'm smack-dab in the old tabula rasa days, bamboozled
    by the books
adults bow over, musing if their eyes light upon
    the white or black spaces,
convinced if I could read like them I'd understand
    the whole shebang.

II

A boyhood later, still wren-small, on the top
    story of The Eagle Printing Company,
I see books pour out and believe that if I fish in
    them
I'll catch the salmon of knowledge, talltaled
    to us at school,
out of the river of words and like Fionn I'll
    taste
my burning hand and abracadabra I'll fathom what's
    below the surface.

III

But if I'm burnt, it's later that day, on my
    first day as pageboy,
dopey from fixing leads, when the devils Fred and
    Dommy typesetting a new book, dispatch
me down to Christy Coughlan on the box floor
    for a tin of striped ink.

I take the bait and watch floors of labouring women
and men flit by, caught in the lift's mesh of Xs,
drowned out by the machines' hullabaloo.
Somehow between floors the elevator conks out
and I'm stuck on my message that I still haven't
cottoned on to.

The Dingbat's Song

I set and reset the Eagle Printing Company
    and the mottled legends that lined its floor,
    struggling with each broken face, dusty beard,
        and chipped shoulder of every fount
    while memory, that proofing make-up man,
keeps returning my bluepencilled dummy galley,
insisting I get each worn body back on its feet.

*

Now I'm stuck like the bastard type, cast
    from that bleeding story that kerns over
    me, and must set myself in this new world,
        quitting the search for those battered
    characters to assure me that I can start
the next hanging paragraph without them
and not make myself a perpetual dingbat.

Ligature

This latent mine—these unlaunch'd voices—passionate powers,
Wrath, argument, or praise, or comic leer, or prayer devout,
(Not nonpareil, brevier, bourgeois, long primer merely,)
These ocean waves arousable to fury and to death,
Or sooth'd to ease and sheeny sun and sleep,
Within the pallid slivers slumbering.

Walt Whitman, 'A Font of Type'

I trekked to the Eagle and the unassuming redbrick
      where you first set *Leaves*, forecasting how you
and all you composed in your time would be
      dismantled and distributed in the composing room
of America before being finally cast aside,
      melted down and recast in the likes of us,
each life set in its unique and sometimes fitting
      fonts and distributed or flung in
the hellbox, turning up again diffused in others.
      But it's our time to set our own lives down,
to select and fix them with our own measure
      in a ligature affixing characters who've gone
before to those close by now and way off in the future

The Broken Type

Consider now the broken and worn types
    thrown without a word in the hellßox of AmeriCa
      like the **BOLD**faced baglady casting
        foul woRdς at the traffic on La Guardia,
or that mackled guy holding a mackled sign
        announcing he has AIDS –– the very letteRs
becoming their own shades — as he begs for change.

And though it's unjust to speak of anyone in terms
    of tyPes, if only we could design a font
      oϝ irrEgulАr TypE faCe made up
        of discarded images and declare it А nEw tyPe.
And by setting their stories in tHis facε,
        we'd retrieve these chАracᵀers care
lessly ρied with the dumping of the capitаl stick.

The Lost Way

to Robert Welch

Snow was general all over Amerikay
as we Kerouaced back from Montreal
trailing our myopic headlights,
nosing through dervishing white smoke.

Somehow miles back we took the wrong turn,
led astray by the Québecois
squabbling in their strange French at the gas station
about which way we should take, reminiscent
of the embarrassing opening scene of *The Quiet Man*,
when John Wayne steps off the train at Innisfree
to a hullabaloo of directing, stage-Irish lalas.

But to give the Canucks the benefit of the doubt,
we may well have got it arseways ourselves,
given how we got lost so often that day, a parody—
a kind of Abbot and Costello Gone to Mars—
of Brendan or Odysseus and their mutinous crews.

Suzanne Vega stereoed 'Calypso'
as we knawvshawled about our families
(our begetters and begotten, no worse than the next,
whose umbilical cords we're still spancelled to)
before we went on to our respective wanderings.

*

In our rent-a-car Chevrolet Troubadour
I seanchaí-ed how I ate the lotus of emigration,
never in a decade of Sundays imagining I'd be
here to stay.
                And like many an *emigrant*
before me I winced at *that* word

28

that once uttered seems to filch me of myself
the way they say a camera steals a soul.
And then there is that stranger word *immigrant*
that I've become and that my tongue that night
stuck on: imimimimegrant: the stammer itself
intimating the meaning.
                You remarked,
freeing my tongue's needle
stuck on its damaged record,
how cúpla dán of mine are a hearkening back,
a kind of grappling for the life buoy's O
of the roads, streets and life of the drowned city
we both hail from, with its perpetual floods.
Its natives are still so blessèdly Irish
they still can't pronounce *th's.* Outsiders,
especially dose from da Pale look down
dare snotty proboscises on our corker Corkonian
dat's not just the closest ding in English to Irish,
but as nare to Elizabedan English freisin
(which is as good an excuse as any for me sonnets)
what wit our *ye* and how we can't pronounce double 'e' r's,
turning, say, *beer* into what all went down to da woods.
But why *like* is dropped into every sentence when dare's nothing
to liken the like to—Ya know, like—we couldn't say.

*

As the windshield wipers said no to the snow
we recalled then like how we laboured on dismal, Pre-Vatican II
Latin, Lenten nights to the men's mission, hardly out
of short pants. A partnership of visiting padres
worked on us like a pair of interrogating New York vice
that must be, since so many of New York's finest are Micks,
where the cops learned questioning techniques.

One spotted guilt in black spots on our tongues,
condemning us to Life in Hell's Alcatraz,
setting us up for his partner
who lured us with immunity, rewards and new identities.

And then there was the hot-footed fretting along Curragh Road,
past Kiely's where we lamped the skimpy bikinied cover girl
of *Titbits* as soon as Mrs Kiely's back was turned,
and where we got the *Victor* and *Hotspur*—
I think on Fridays—after our Das doled out
our weekly pocket money of an English or Irish
threepenny bit. Which was which I could never tell.
I can still recall the forking-out, print-inked hands
of my father, setting gentle words in me, his impress,
and me swearing I'd be a compositor like him when I grew up.

We'd bribe cogs on undone homework mornings
with the currency of Trigger Bars, lucky bags, gob stoppers,
acid drops, Hadji Beys, donkey's gudge, Taytos,
Flakes, Thomson's custard slices, liquorice snakes
black as the tongues of our souls . . .
Though I suspect you, being brighter than mise, gave cogs,
and for nought as is your nature. But how could we
out-smart-aleck the holy terrors of our childhoods?:
Sister Benedict, Brother Dermot, Dantro, Leo . . . all
all too ready to root out the dodos, amadáns,
goms, slow ones, with endless spelling tests
and the Tuiseal ginideach of Irish grammar.
They turned us from our natural tongue
with their regime, more than any tallystick,
always ready with the cat-of-nine-tails of their bataí
while us cats perpetually ran out of our nine lives.
And now the cats are out of the bag,
but we'll let all that catty, clergy-bashing old hat go.

Besides there were good ones too: Sister Patrick,
Brother Pius, Fabian and Brother William—who chucked it,
and according to the bible of rumour, shacked up with a nun—
and oh, John O'Shea who could read poetry aloud
better than anyone and still can and does . . .
all those nourishing souls who blessed those hand-wringing days
and sent us on our not-so-merry, merry ways.

*

Oh but I keep getting lost like our drive that day,
as if being lost is the actual right way,
taking our cue from the likes of Christy Columbus, Brendan,
Odysseus and Wrong Way Corrigan: all that misdirected crew,
whose wrong ways turned out right.
Quod erat demonstrandum: the right way
being the lost way and the long way round
being the only way home, it being home.

*

All I set out to say was what has stayed with me
of that day and that drive home is how I had,
corny as it sounds, a sort of epiphany:
the snow scattering into the lights
were not the tatters of a torn exercise page that correcting
Brother Dermot, Sister Benedict or any of the poetry heads
tore in disgust and cast all abaa in the darkening classroom
that falling snow reminded me of earlier—
No: rather it was the opposite of the sins
of our childhood that blew over our tongues
and souls like the soot of bonfire night,
coating all the windows of our city.
The snow was manna falling within us,

as good a symbol as any of the nourishing company
and gab of our day, knowing with all the darkness
crowding our vision that we were blessed too
what with our families, friends and the miracle of miracles:
poetry, shagging poetry, I kid you not,
lucky enough to have come this way.

The snow fell in the silence that poetry
falls with as it drops a beneficence of
white calmness around us in the darkness.

*

The next thing I recall as we snail-paced down
from the white White Mountains was finally finding
our bearings at a crossroads with a shellityhorn spired,
picture postcard New England church to the right of us,
somewhere near Morrisville that, while my friend
Chuck lived there, I nicknamed Nowheresville.

At first we thought there was something terribly wrong,
an accident, seeing what looked like a father and son
out of their pick-up, sprawling at the roadside,
moving their arms and legs as if writhing in pain.
But then it dawned on me they were making snow angels,
signing their body's X signature in a snow mound.
They might have been aping early pioneers of flight
or even Daedalus and Icarus making a myth of that myth,
finally copping that their escape plan is for the birds
and never again wanting to leave the blessèd ground.

We Will Not Play the Harp Backward Now, No

If in Ireland
they play the harp backward at need
Marianne Moore, 'Spenser's Ireland'

We, a bunch of greencard Irish,
   vamp it under the cathedral arches
   of Brooklyn Bridge that's strung like a harp.
But we'll not play
the harp backward now, harping on
     about those Micks who fashioned
this American wind lyre
and about the scores
     who landed on Ellis Island
or, like us, at Kennedy and dispersed
through this open sesame land

in different directions like the rays
   of Liberty's crown, each ray set
   against the other, forming a wedge or caret.
We'll refrain from inserting
how any of us craved for the old country
     and in our longing, composed a harp,
pipe, porter and colleen Tir na nOg.
And if we play
     the harp right way round now
we'll reveal another side of the story
told like the secret of Labraid the Exile: how

some, at least, found a native genius for union
    here and where like the Earl Gerald,
    who turned himself into a stag
and a green-eyed cat
of the mountain, many of us
        learned the trick
of turning ourselves into ourselves,
free in the fe fiada anonymity
        of America. Here
we could flap the horse's ears
of our singularity and not have to fear,

nor hide from the all-seeing Irish
    small town, blinking evil eyes—
    Nor does this landscape play that unheard,
but distinctly audible
mizzling slow air
        that strickens us with the plaintive notes
of the drawn-out tragedy
of the old country's sorry history.
            No, we'll not play the harp backward
anymore, keeping in mind the little people's harp
and how those who hear it never live long afterward.

THE HELLBOX

The Hellbox

When push comes to shove, more than anything
I didn't want to feel a foreigner
in my own, what would you call it, homeland?,
or just the *Old Country*, as here they label
anywhere across the drink and that I still,
circa a decade later, surprise myself
in casual conversation by calling *home*.
I forget how that small boat of an island
jettisoned so many of us so readily,
its flotsam and jetsam, to stay afloat.

Everything was turning strangely strange,
unable to land work that would allow the muse
a sliver of space to descend and work,
not to speak of how belovèd souls began to kick
the bucket while others jumped ship before us,
opting for the lesser ill of feeling foreign
somewhere foreign rather than at so-called home.

And then there was the city itself changing
so hell for leather, even if it was for the better,
that some of us felt oddly abandoned. Our one-time, dark
side streets and alleys are now trendy shopping thoroughfares:
Paradise Place, French Church Street, Half Moon Street,
Carey's Lane where after Kojak's Nightclub
I pulled off the occasional guilt-ridden feel
and even managed the odd fumbling dry ride.
And I'll say little of how aliens like Burgerlands
and McDonald's took over main streets and buildings
in the continuous sci-fi movie of our century,
nor about the twilight zone, routing roads
that the Cork Corporation calls *Da Super Highway*,
motoring over fields, woods and railway lines that still
hoot and whistle inside me down the sleepers of the years

and where we played the Easter Rising. I was
fierce Pearse, wheelchair Connolly and Cork's own Big Fella,
never Joseph *Mary* Plunkett, wearing my Billy the Kid cowboy hat
pinned to one side Volunteer-style; though somewhat reluctantly
I took my turn at being an executing Tommy.

On other days we played Cowboys and Indians.
I was always the lone redskin brave
having written in my Santa letter one misdirected Christmas
for an Indian suit with a set of Big Chief feathers
colourful as a macaw or a bird of paradise,
spotted in Kilgrew's Toy Shop that's shot now also;
all gone Baker's John along with the aroma
of Thomson's bakery rising like dough over the Lee.
The mane of on-the-warpath feathers trailed gloriously
or flapped mid-air all those times I was hunted and fired at
as I rode Injun style, wishing there were more Indians
and I didn't all the time have to be the sole baddy
and that one of the cavalry would swap outfits,
and let me join the paleface, but no one ever did.
And who else could they chase? I've this notion that
that lonesome whooping, bow and arrow Apache,
always staying one step ahead of the posse,
eventually camped way up the line in a hideout
writing his smoke signal poems on the sky.

But I probably would have stayed put and got by
if it wasn't for some wan, some female, some cailín,
some fine half, some fla, some paragon, some Helen
of Lennox's Chipper, some Rose of Tralee, some jo,
some comely maiden, some looker, some Veronica—how
could four syllables mean so much?—chucking me, ditching me,
whooping me, giving me the boot, the elbow, the old hi-di-ho.
She left me in the lurch, up the creek, up

the Sewanee without a paddle, without a prayer,
pissing into the forlorn poetic gale of a wind.
Though I've a hunch I schemed the sequence of events,
so I wouldn't have to be the guilty party,
left with the dirty work of calling the shots
when the shit hits the fan of those terrible words
that were the opposite of this buckaroo's marriage proposal.
And like any true troubadour (you know what that shower's like:
they'd shoot their grandmothers for the sake of a haiku),
I was sniffing out unrequited, gone with the wind love poems.

Yet I still muse about those happy
never after, to love, cherish and disobey days.
But what's the use? Shur didn't I discard all that
that morning Ger and Lou and Tom saw me off
at Dublin airport, a mite craw-sick
after my American wake, lugging a backpack
mostly of books that was so heavy I keeled over
on my back at the arrival doors
that went on in a spasm of opening and closing
waiting for me to pass through: harbinger
of the coming years? I lay on my back
like an insect unable to turn itself over.
And all our convulsions of laughter didn't help:
I nearly wet myself. I can still see Ger
in stitches and all the passersby steering clear.
And then when the check-in lady informed me
I was over the limit I wasn't sure if she was referring
to me or the bag that was as heavy as something in me
though I let on nothing as I waved Hasta la vista
to my dear, high jinks, roughhousing, boozing,
poetry gun-slinging, old amigos: acting the man's man,
letting on nothing as if I was stepping on the bus
for the day down to Cobh or Youghal or Cronin's in Crosser.

And their ghosts still wave the ghost of myself
off through the mundane Cerberus of security
from that country that I was nothing more or less than,
more than less of, that's me for as long as me is.
But like Veronica, my sometime old doll,
my whilom homeland had turned strange and all wrong.

And then in this other country, in this other story:
finding myself suddenly in floods late at night
in the leaba alone, or in an empty afternoon cinema,
for sweet nothing, for that island that I longed for.
I yearned not for the American Irish fantasy:
the isle of jolly, stroppy drinkers; Tir na nOg;
Ballyshamrock; Innisleprechaun; the honeyed trap
of the reminiscing emigrant. But rather I hankered for
certain belovèd people; for the street friendliness
that I thought in the old days before leaving entered my noggin,
was a Board Failte gimmick; for the landscape that as much
as it stifled us with its dinnshenachas of suffering,
also rooted us in a place, in an order;
not to speak of longing for the refuge
of a real pub and a proper pint of porter.
In such a state I remind myself how that island, that Thule
of another time, had given me and others short shrift,
expelling us like the Children of Lir,
not giving us the steam off its piss.

But where to, where am I? Only an hour or so ago
that same blue-in-the-face question struck again
on sidewalks few ever walk or even rollerblade,
along the typical characterless automobile-whizzing strip
that could have been anywhere, excusing the snow,
all the way down to the handle of Miami
and across the States that get bigger and squarer

as they nudge their way to funky Californ-i-ay:
miles of malls, hotels, motels, strip joints,
Roy Rogers, Haircuts For Less, Blockbuster Videos,
Ben Franklins, Frugal Franks, Pepper's Memphis Barbecue,
Dunkin Donuts, drive-in banks, drive-in this, drive-in that . . .

I stuck my pen like a flag into this twilight zone:
an Irish Amundsen at the poetry Pole of the province
where all emigrants naturally land, except that I am Scott too,
lost and laden down with experiments,
settling into the tent that last Antarctic night
with his crew, always only one mangy mile from home.

*

But to hell with all that American waking, that bull,
that myth–making crap that I probably also rigged
like the Veronica caper and mostly for the sake
of venturing to discover some new way of saying
the same old rigamarole: birth and death and everything
sandwiched between and that I have trouble fitting
my mouth around or into like one of those typical
colossal American sandwiches no one bats an eye at here.
And yes everything is larger anseo. Look,
even me own poems are getting blasted bigger.
I'm cross-fertilizing my regular, leprechaun-small strain
with the crazy American variant as if the Irish to-mat-o
was crossed with the whale of the Yankee to-mate-o
that itself looks like one of those radioactive mutants
of Chernobyl along with the likes of two headed calves
that my old comrade, Adi anti-nuclear Roche, photographed
to show the world. O Adi save the world for us. Gather the ill
winds of Chernobyl into the Aeolus leather bag of your will
and blow us home to the home of your dreams that are ours too,

sans thick men undoing its knot. You say there's hope still.
Outside my window a jostling bevy of chickadees laugh.
These flitting characters poke their mugs into the O
of the underside of our pendulum birdfeeding globe,
maybe exactly where the French test their arrogance now.
The seed falls from the top half of the hemisphere
of our glass like sand in an egg-timer. Already time
has run out for so many creatures, so many
now per second, so many we haven't the foggiest notion of.
Oh how can we turn the timer of the world around?
And how can poetry Aidi-in and make it happen?
And Adi, even if your entreaties to make love
not war are cliché, your vision aint. Even now
in my mind's ear I hear your gusto, revivifying
every cliché in the book. Say you're in solidarity,
in sisterhood with this. Say Maaan O Man.
Say, brother, this is the awesomeness of awesome.
Say it's not just you're in it, but we all are.
And as you mouth clichés in praise of this,
say loathsome clichés are only a way of not being alone.
Say this is cliché and that I know how they love cliché, even
as cliché dulleth life. I know they've enough of aloneness.
Let us break through and come out
the other side. Let's all be together in them for once.
And oh I hereby declareth on this the tenth Day
of the tenth month in the year of Himself or Herself,
the Great Compositor, nineteen hundred and pied
ninety-five anno damini, thrown like all the other broken
and worn days into the hellbox of this century,
that *awesome* poetry should be dumped. Say I want this to be
the most laughable, spoilt job ever to be set down,
that it will be killed before it's read
and thus be the be-all and end-all truth,
since we'll all be forgotten sooner

rather than Shakespeare and even he'll eventually get dossed.
And then being the most arrogant of shams I want the other
side of the truth of this story: how since this sublunar life
of ours is such a pain, so imperfect in one way or another,
that the more imperfect words are, the truer they are and
the truer they are the greater. Thus spake a Grecian saucepan.
Ergo, this clichéd pontificating litany in one fell swoop
is the greatest, awesomest piece ever written along with all
the zillions of cat-melodeon poems published in the zillions
of lousy newspapers and mags across the poetry globe,
out McGonagalling the McGonagall himself like that Canuck bard,
Jim McIntyre, who composed 'Ode on the Mammoth Cheese' to one
humungous cheddar. The first of a langer-load of verses goeth:

We have seen thee, queen of cheese
Lying quietly at your ease,
Gently fanned by evening breeze,
Thy fair form no fly dare seize.

Everyone laughed at him. He thought he was great. And he was,
he was. Jimmy, old stock, you can finally rest easy.
You're the greatest. We all are. Everyone with duck-all talent
is finally coming true. We hereby decree all the crappy poets
from here to poetry's Timbucktoo are greater than all
the age's Willies and Willas—And what, pray,
is *great* poetry anyway? *You gotta have heart,*
(now everyone sing along)
                                    Miles and miles of heart.

                        Oh it's nice to be a genius of course,
                        But keep that old horse
                        Before the cart . . .

43

As the dark wood said to the Lion: If I were you I'd turn
back now: *You gotta have heart,* (now all together again)
                    Miles and miles of heart . . .
But outside poetry's ticker, if the power of suggestion,
leaving so much to the imagination, is the chief attribute of
a poem, then Dorothy of the delving cleavage you're *some* poem.
Oh when will the nine Dorothy's descend and blow me?
O Jesus, there's been enough ducking and deprecating.
What about the Muses down on 42nd Street,
the ladies of my blue fantasies that come to life
in the confessional of peep show booths,
stripping the lingerie of suggestion
slip by agonizing slinky slip, dancing
into the poetry nip? Please talk dirty to me.
Sure I'm tipping. 'Easy honey, easy.
What's your fancy? Titties or a hand job?' . . .
And I have just left down a dream of a poem:
'El Journey' and Sappho came beside me . . .
and without a word I went with her

down down down . . .
                    Then to my horror I could see to each
                    nipple some had clipped a limpet shape—
                    suckling darknesses—while others had their arms
                    weighed down, making terrible pietas.

                    She took my sleeve and said to me "be careful . . .

"what you have seen is beyond speech,
beyond song, only not beyond love;

"remember it, you will remember it . . ."
And the peep show's window slid shut
harsh as love . . . *nothing was changed; nothing more clear . . .*
the year was late . . . and I wept—
my eyes have seen what my hand did.

44

And yes I know I've blown this, but to hell with poetry:
life's more important. I could go on
and on adding forever to this mumbo jumbo sandwich.
But I better wrap up, finish my ranting and rambling ravings.
Has everyone high tailed it? Is there anyone there?
Was there ever any soul there? Is that snoring I hear?

*

All I want is not simply to parrot American voices,
      reminding me of how immigrants learned
a new tongue from mimicking gramophone songs
      and following theatre stars from show to show,
pronouncing actors' lines, rhythms, always a fraction behind,
      till they knew every word, so much so, according to
Ondaatje, that when Wayne Burnett dropped dead
      on stage a Sicilian butcher in the audience took over.

No siree, I eschew such mimicry and want to be poetry's
      Temelcoff, who so desperately learned a new tongue
that he had translation dreams where trees not just changed
      their names, but their looks and character,
men answered in falsetto and dogs spoke in the street.
      More than anything I want my utterance to become the stuff
of such dreams, while remaining always human, open, up front.

I'm the cocky young cleric coming to St Brendan's door
      refusing to leave till I've played the music of the world:
more pleasing to me any day than the saint's dazzling angel
      who, from the altar on high, drew the bow of its beak
across the harp of its wing and played a tricksy, highbrow
      lay that was so ethereal, Brendan forever afterwards plugged
his ears to any human harp. A pox on such angelic harping.
      Let my fingers pluck the common note of an open harp.

But who am I kidding? Where is that down-to-earth angel
    who Mossy, fellow agent of the muse, swore is sooner rather
than later going to turn up to give poetry the kiss of life
    and 'blow us all out of the water' as we mused
one night about our own strains and how the general state
    of poesy is at a low ebb. So where are you, you human angel,
or whatever you are? Give us a stave, a melody, an air.
    Who are we bluffing with our efforts? Oh come on out.
We love you Buster. Blow us all out of the water.

OXFORD POETS

Fleur Adcock
Moniza Alvi
Joseph Brodsky
Basil Bunting
Tessa Rose Chester
Daniela Crăsnaru
Greg Delanty
Michael Donaghy
Keith Douglas
D. J. Enright
Roy Fisher
Ida Affleck Graves
Ivor Gurney
David Harsent
Gwen Harwood
Anthony Hecht
Zbigniew Herbert
Tobias Hill
Thomas Kinsella
Brad Leithauser
Derek Mahon
Jamie McKendrick

Sean O'Brien
Alice Oswald
Peter Porter
Craig Raine
Zsuzsa Rakovszky
Christopher Reid
Stephen Romer
Eva Salzman
Carole Satyamurti
Peter Scupham
Jo Shapcott
Penelope Shuttle
Goran Simić
Anne Stevenson
George Szirtes
Grete Tartler
Edward Thomas
Charles Tomlinson
Marina Tsvetaeva
Chris Wallace-Crabbe
Hugo Williams